Reflections

Reflections

by

Wayne Evans

Everlasting Publishing
Yakima, Washington
USA

Reflections
by
Wayne Evans

Cover photograph & design
by Jahla Brown

ISBN-13: 978-0-9983858-2-2

First Edition
Everlasting Publishing
P.O. Box 1061
Yakima, WA 98907
USA

THIS BOOK IS DEDICATED TO
MY FAMILY AND FRIENDS...
MY TRUE INSPIRATIONS.

In Memory

Benny
Tony
Gerald
Wilbert

Gone... never forgotten

REFLECTIONS

"11"

IT'S EASY TO REMEMBER HIS NAME
YOU SEE MINE IS THE VERY SAME.

A NICE MAN WITH A HEART OF GOLD
I'M GLAD TO WATCH AS HE GROWS OLD.

HELPFUL TO OTHERS IN EVERY WAY
A VIRTUE THAT I HOPE WILL STAY.

I PRAY FOR HIM EVERY NIGHT
AND HOPE HE'LL DO WHAT HE KNOWS IS RIGHT.

I GUESS YOU KNOW WHEN ALL IS DONE
I'M MIGHTY PROUD TO CALL HIM SON.

I LOVE HIM MUCH AS YOU CAN SEE
REMINDS ME SO MUCH OF ME.

WSE1

ALPHA – OMEGA

THE BEGINNING AND THE END
FROM INTRODUCTION TO THE MASTER
TO THE UNDERSTANDING OF A FRIEND.

THE FIRST TO SEEK, THE FIRST TO REAP
I'VE FOUND A FRIEND, HE'S MINE TO KEEP.

WSE1

AMERICA, THE BEAUTIFUL.

AMERICA, THE BEAUTIFUL, LAND OF THE FREE
THE ONE PLACE ON EARTH WE ALL WANT TO BE.

AMERICA, THE BEAUTIFUL... OH WHERE HAVE YOU GONE?
YOU LEFT US STRANDED... WE FEEL SO ALONE.

THEY'RE KILLING OUR CHILDREN AS THEY TRY TO LEARN
GUNS ALL OVER... SO LITTLE CONCERN.

COPS KILLING PEOPLE ALL OVER THE PLACE
SO MUCH VIOLENCE... SUCH A DISGRACE.

THE "DIFFERENT" ARE SCOLDED AND TOLD WHO TO BE
I THOUGHT WE ALL LIVED IN THE "LAND OF THE FREE."

WAGES ARE STAGNANT WHILE STOCK MARKETS SOAR
THE RICH GETTING RICHER, THE POOR STAYING POOR.

ALL ALONG I THOUGHT WE WERE "GREATER"
NOW FEAR FOR YOUR LIFE AT THE MOVIE THEATER.

AMERICA THE BEAUTIFUL, BE ALL THAT YOU CAN
AND LET'S BE KINDER TO OUR FELLOW MAN.

WSE1

ARNOLD

GREAT OUTDOORSMAN AND ANGLER
BUT EVEN A BETTER FRIEND.

THE TYPE YOU PRAY WILL REMAIN
THERE UNTIL THE VERY END.

ONCE YOU MEET HIM
YOU'LL KNOW HE'S FOR REAL.

IT'S GREAT TO HAVE A FRIEND
LIKE ARNOLD CASTILLE!

WSE1

AVIS

SHE'S AS SWEET AS SHE COULD BE
BUT THEN SHE IS VERY SPECIAL TO ME.

I LOVE HER SO AND ALWAYS WILL
TO SEE HER SMILE IS SUCH A THRILL.

I WATCH HER THROUGH LIFE SHE GOES
I WISH THE BEST AND CURSE THE WOES.

FOR HER I'D CHALLENGE THE WHOLE-WIDE WORLD
MY DARLING SWEETHEART... MY "LITTLE" GIRL.

THEY SAY FATHERS LOVE DAUGHTERS TOO MUCH
BUT I NEVER SEEM TO LISTEN TO SUCH.

I LOVE HER DEARLY, EACH BRAID AND CURL
MY DARLING SWEETHEART... MY "LITTLE" GIRL.

WSE1

AWE

I DREAD THE DAY THAT I WAS BORN
TO LIVE A LIFE OF SHAME AND SCORN.

TO LAUGH, TO CRY, TO LIVE, TO DIE
TO LOOK BEYOND THE ENDLESS SKY.

TO LIVE IN A WORLD OF HATE AND FEAR
TO LOSE THE THINGS I HOLD SO DEAR.

WSE1

BENNY

HE WAS MY FRIEND, THE BEST OF MANY
HE CALLED ME "BUBBA," I CALLED HIM BENNY.

A GENTLE SOUL WITH LOVE TO SPARE
HE'S THE ONE YOU KNEW WOULD SHARE.

WE LOVED TO CAMP, LIKE MANY OTHERS
WE DRANK, WE TALKED, WE WERE BROTHERS.

THE PLACES WE WENT, THE FUN WE HAD
I MISS HIM MUCH, IT MAKES ME SAD.

I THINK OF THE THINGS WE NEVER HAVE DONE
LIKE MEETING AT "FOUR CORNERS" UNDER THE SUN.

I KNOW AGAIN OUR PATHS WILL CROSS
THEN MAYBE I WON'T FEEL SUCH LOSS.

5/1/2016

WSE1

CHRISTINE

SHE'S MY SON'S QUEEN, SWEET CHRISTINE
A LOVING PERSON... NEVER MEAN.

ALWAYS BUSY... DOES MORE THAN SHE OUGHTA
I'M VERY PROUD TO CALL HER DAUGHTER.

I LOVE TO SEE HER SMILING FACE
SHE TAKES IT WITH HER EVERY PLACE.

SHE CAN SHOP AND SHOP UNTIL YOU DROP...
FINDING TREASURES, DON'T EVER STOP.

HER PERSEVERANCE INSPIRES US ALL...
NO HILL TOO HIGH, NO DEED TOO SMALL.

SHE'S LOVING, KIND AND ALWAYS SWEET
A BETTER PERSON YOU WILL NEVER MEET.

IF YOU KNOW HER, YOU KNOW WHAT I MEAN
MY SON'S QUEEN... SWEET CHRISTINE!!!

WSE1

CLOVIS

YOU MAY NOT KNOW THIS
I HAVE A FRIEND NAMED CLOVIS.

ALWAYS "DAPPER" AND LOOKING GOOD
YOU'D NEVER KNOW HE'S FROM THE "HOOD."

BEEN ALL OVER, SOME PLACES TWICE
ALWAYS FRIENDLY, ALWAYS NICE.

IN THE BIG HOUSE, HIGH ON THE HILL
YET DOWN-TO-EARTH AND STRIVING STILL.

WE'VE KNOWN EACH OTHER FOR FORTY YEARS
SHARED MANY LAUGHS AND SOMETIMES TEARS.

DON'T REMEMBER THE DATE, OR EVEN THE YEAR
WE SMOKED A "JOINT" AT TONY'S -ON-THE-PIER.

I WISH HIM WELL AS HE TRAVELS THE WORLD
WHILE BY HIS SIDE, HIS FAVORITE "GIRL."

BE SAFE, MY FRIEND, TILL WE MEET AGAIN
WHEN I CAN HEAR STORIES OF WHERE YOU'VE BEEN.

WSE1

CONFESSIONS

CONFESSIONS OF MY LOVE FOR YOU
TELLING HOW I LOVE YOU TRUE.
THE WONDERFUL THINGS YOU DO WITH GLEE
THE LOVE AND HAPPINESS YOU SHARE WITH ME.

IT'S ALL OF THIS OF WHICH I SPEAK
MY FRIEND, MY PAL, IT'S YOU I SEEK.
TO LOVE AND HOLD FOREVER MORE
TO SHARE, PROTECT, TO SHIELD AND ADORE.

TOGETHER I KNOW OUR HORIZONS WILL EXPAND
WE'LL BEAT THE ODDS... WHATEVER THEY DEMAND.
WE'LL BE HAPPY, SECURE, AT PEACE TOGETHER
THERE WILL BE NO STORM OUR LOVE WON'T WEATHER.

WSE1

DAUGHTERS

A FATHER'S FIRST LOVE, MY "LITTLE" GIRL
NOTHING'S TOO MUCH, NOT EVEN THE WORLD.

HAS MY HEART, BODY AND SOUL
STILL MY "BABY," NO MATTER HOW OLD.

LOVE HER TO THE DAY I DIE
NEVER WANT TO SEE HER CRY.

I HOPE THE WORLD WILL BE AS GOOD
AS WE HOPE AND KNOW IT SHOULD.

MASTER OF ALL THE WORLDS
I PRAY THAT YOU PROTECT MY GIRLS.

WSE1

E.J.

A BETTER COOK YOU WILL NOT MEET.
THE MEALS WILL SWEEP YOU OFF YOUR FEET.

SHE'S KIND, GENEROUS AND ALWAYS FAIR.
IF YOU EVER NEED HER... SHE'LL BE THERE.

SHE'S KNOWLEDGEABLE ON ALMOST EVERYTHING
FROM PLANTS IN THE GROUND...
TO BIRDS ON THE WING.

TO SPEND TIME WITH HER IS SUCH A PLEASURE
HER FRIENDSHIP'S VALUE IS HARD TO MEASURE.

A SPECIAL PERSON FROM BEGINNING TO END
I'M SO PROUD TO CALL HER MY FRIEND.

WSE1

EMOTIONS

EMOTIONS, EMOTIONS, OH HOW CAN I CONTROL?
SOMETIMES THE FEELINGS LEAVE ME SO COLD.

UNCONTROLLABLE, OUT ON THE WILD.
EMOTIONS SOMETIMES RUN FAIRLY MILD.

I CAN'T BOX THEM IN, REALLY, NO NEED TO TRY
THEY'RE WITH ME FROM BIRTH TO THE DAY I DIE.

I'LL LIVE WITH THEM THE BEST I CAN,
LOVE ALL OTHERS, BE MY OWN MAN.

WSE1

EVAN

HE WAS OUR PERFECT GIFT FROM HEAVEN
MOM DECIDED TO CALL HIM EVAN.

HIS BRAIN IS HIS MOST VALUABLE TOOL
DOING WELL IN LIFE AND GREAT IN SCHOOL.

HE'S HIS GRANDMA'S PRIDE AND JOY
SHE THINKS OF HIM AS HER "LITTLE BOY."

HE'S GROWING INTO A FINE YOUNG MAN
ALWAYS DOING THE BEST HE CAN.

WE WISH HIM WELL IN ALL HE DOES
AND PRAY HE FINDS HIS OWN TRUE LOVES.

HE LOVES HIS "PAPA" AND "GRANDMA" TOO
THERE IS NOTHING FOR HIM WE WOULD NOT DO.

SO, CLIMB AND CLIMB TO REACH THE TOP
NO MATTER WHAT HAPPENS... NEVER STOP.

WSE1

FOSTER

WE CAME TO CELEBRATE YOUR LIFE
AND OFFER COMFORT TO YOUR WIFE.

I MISS YOU MUCH, MY FRIEND SO DEAR
OH, HOW I WISH YOU STILL WERE HERE.

SO PURE OF HEART AND SHARP OF MIND
CONSIDERATE OF OTHERS, ALWAYS KIND.

WISE BEYOND YOUR MANY YEARS
I LEARNED FROM YOU TO FACE MY FEARS.

HONEST, FAIR, BRIGHT AND CHEERY
FULL OF LIFE, NEVER WEARY.

WE CELEBRATE THE HEARTS YOU TOUCHED
REST IN PEACE, WE MISS YOU MUCH.

WSE1

GERALD

COULD HIT THE BALL THREE HUNDRED YARDS
GOOD AT "BONES" ... BETTER AT CARDS.

GREAT AT SPORTS, NEVER SAT IN THE BLEACHERS
WATCHED HIM BECOME
ONE OF GOLF'S BEST TEACHERS.

A SENSE OF HUMOR TO MATCH NO OTHER
HE MAKES ME LAUGH... I LOVE MY BROTHER.

AT HOME IN NATURE... HE LOVES ALL CREATURES
HIS LOVE FOR CANINES IS ONE OF HIS FEATURES.

I MISS MY BROTHER ON THE "OTHER" COAST
SO, I'LL RAISE MY GLASS AND PROPOSE A TOAST.

"HERE'S TO US AND THE GOOD TIMES WE'VE HAD
SEEING YOU AGAIN WILL MAKE ME GLAD."

FORTY-YEAR FRIENDSHIPS ARE HARD TO FIND
THANKS TO YOU FOR BEING SO KIND.

WSE1

GETTING "OLD"

AS WE AGE AND START TO GET OLD
THERE'S STILL A STORY TO BE TOLD.

OF FRIENDSHIPS AND MEMORIES OF THE PAST
OH MY, TIME HAS MOVED SO FAST.

WHEN WE WERE YOUNG
AND THE APPLE OF THEIR EYE
WE THOUGHT WE'D LIVE FOREVER AND NEVER DIE.

GOOD TIMES AND FUN WE ALWAYS HAD
AND WHEN THEY GO IT LEAVES US SAD.

WE DON'T LIVE FOREVER... WE KNOW THIS WELL
AND SO, THIS STORY WE MUST TELL.

WE LOVE OUR FRIENDS
AND THE JOY THEY BROUGHT
THE THINGS SHARED... THE LESSONS TAUGHT.

SO, WHEN IT'S TIME TO SAY GOODBYE
LIFT YOUR HEAD AND DRY YOUR EYE.

THINK OF THE THINGS THAT MADE YOU LAUGH
REMEMBER, LIFE IS FULL... IT'S NEVER HALF.

TREAT YOUR FRIENDS GENTLY
BECAUSE YOU NEVER KNOW
WHEN IT'S TIME FOR ONE OF US TO GO.

WSE1

IAN

YOU WILL KNOW HIM WHEN YOU SEE HIM
A NICE YOUNG GUY NAMED IAN.

SMART AS A BEE, STRONG AS A TREE
HE MEANS THE WHOLE WORLD TO ME.

HIS HEART IS THE SIZE OF AN OCEAN
HIS BODY AND MIND ALWAYS IN MOTION.

HIS LOVE FOR OTHERS IS PLAIN TO SEE
HE LOVES THE WORLD AND YOU AND ME.

I'M SURE HE WILL GROW INTO QUITE A MAN
HE HELPS OTHERS AS MUCH AS HE CAN.

HE'S A SPECIAL YOUNG MAN AS YOU CAN SEE
BLESS HIM, GOD, HOLD HIM CLOSE TO THEE.

WSE1

IT'S OUR "THING"

WE E-MAIL, TEXT, TWEET AND STREAM
WE DON'T TALK TO EACH OTHER
OR SHARE A DREAM.

INJUSTICE HERE, MISERY THERE
SOUNDS LIKE HOPE HAS NO CHANCE.
DROP THE ATTITUDE, STAND UP TALL
AND PLEASE... PULL UP THOSE PANTS.

WE ARE NOT WEAK, THE FUTURE'S NOT BLEAK
I THINK WE'LL BE JUST FINE.
SO, FIND YOUR NICHE IN THIS WORLD OF OURS
WHILE I DO MY BEST TO FIND MINE!

WSE1

KINGSLEY LAKE

IT'S PERFECTLY ROUND
AND THE WATER IS CLEAR
YOU CAN ONLY EXPERIENCE IT
BY BEING HERE.

IT'S TWO AND A HALF MILES
IN ANY DIRECTION
ANOTHER EXAMPLE
OF NATURE'S PERFECTION.

THE FISHING'S GOOD
AND THE SKIING, TOO
A WONDERFUL PLACE
WITH THE PERFECT VIEW.

HERONS AND EGRETS
SEARCHING FOR FOOD
TURTLES AND DUCKS
TO SOOTHE YOUR MOOD.

THE SUNRISES AND SUNSETS
ARE BEAUTIFUL TO SEE
THERE'S NO OTHER PLACE
I'D RATHER BE.

WSE1

LET'S TALK

EVEN BEFORE WE LEARN TO WALK
WE'RE BLESSED WITH THE GIFT OF TALK.

WE MUMBLE ABOUT IN CONSTANT CHATTER
LEARNING TO SAY, "WHAT'S THE MATTER"?

ALL THROUGH OUR YOUTH WE TALK TO OURSELVES
WE'VE EVEN BEEN KNOWN TO TALK TO ELVES.

SO WHY, WITH ALL OUR EDUCATION
DO WE MISS THE POINT OF COMMUNICATION?

WSE1

MIKE

IT'S FIVE O'CLOCK FRIDAY... A TIME THAT I LIKE
I GET TO BOND WITH MY GOOD FRIEND, MIKE.

WE'RE MILES APART IF SPACE IS YOUR MEASURE
YET OUR "WARM-UPS" ARE SUCH A PLEASURE.

THOUGH THE CONVERSATION IS NEVER HEATED
THE THINGS WE SAY CAN'T BE REPEATED.

A JOKE OR TWO, A SIP OF WINE
ALL OF A SUDDEN, ALL IS FINE.

SOLVING THE WORLD'S PROBLEMS
MAKING SURE THEY'RE STRAIGHT
AND THAT SHOULD HOLD US
TO MONDAY AT EIGHT.

WSE1

MY FRIEND

I AWOKE THIS MORNING WITH A TEAR IN MY EYE
I WONDERED ALOUD, "WHAT MADE ME CRY?"

THEN I RECALLED THE DREAM I'D HAD
IT WAS OF MY FRIEND, IT MADE ME SAD.

I REMEMBERED THE TIMES WE'D HAD TOGETHER
THE SUNNY DAYS, THE INCLIMATE WEATHER.

THE LAKES WE FISHED WERE SO MUCH FUN
UP IN THE MORNING BEFORE THE SUN.

OUT IN THE BOAT WITH TIME TO SPARE
SO MUCH FUN... YOU HAD TO BE THERE.

IF HE WERE HERE, I'M SURE HE'D SAY,
"YOU LET THE BIG ONE GET AWAY."

THE DAY WILL COME, I'M SURE YOU'LL WAIT
YOU'LL DO THE FISHING, I'LL CUT THE BAIT.

SO, CAST YOUR LINE AND KEEP IT TIGHT
I KNOW FOR SURE WE'LL BE ALRIGHT.

WSE1

MY GUIDING LIGHT

INTO MY LIFE CAME ALL THE THINGS
THAT MADE ME FEEL COMPLETE.
AND AS I GREW LIFE REVEALED
BOTH BITTER AND THE SWEET.

LOVE TAUGHT ME HOW TO CHERISH
BUT LOVE I HAD TO LEARN.
LOVE SHOWED ME PEACE AND FREEDOM
BUT LEFT HAPPINESS FOR ME TO EARN.

LOVE GAVE ME EYES TO SEE
THE CONTRAST BETWEEN WRONG AND RIGHT
MAY THE LOVE YOU'VE GIVEN ME…
REMAIN MY GUIDING LIGHT.

WSE1

MY LOVE

TO THE LOVE OF MY LIFE
MY FRIEND, MY PARTNER, MY WIFE.

YOU BRING ME HAPPINESS, YOU BRING ME CHEER!
I LOVE YOU MORE YEAR AFTER YEAR.

THE WARM FEELING OF YOUR CONSTANT PRESENCE
FULFILLS MY LIFE AND MAKES IT PLEASANT.

I'LL ALWAYS LOVE YOU, AS YOU WELL KNOW
AND THROUGH THE YEARS OUR LOVE WILL GROW.

ALWAYS AND FOREVER,

WSE1

MY SISTER

MY LOVE, MY LIFE, MY SISTER

I REMEMBER HAVING A SISTER
BEFORE I REALIZED I HAD PARENTS.

SHE HAS PLAYED A PIVOTAL ROLE
IN MY DEVELOPMENT,
VISION OF THE WORLD,
HOW THINGS WORK AND WHY.

A PORTRAIT OF COURAGE, GRACE AND PRIDE
STRONG AS NEEDED, ALWAYS BY MY SIDE.

A GREAT SENSE Of HUMOR,
I CAN STILL MAKE HER LAUGH
IF I HAD TWO PARTS,
SHE'D BE MY BETTER HALF.

I GUESS YOU'D REALLY HAVE TO BE ME
TO APPRECIATE A SISTER SUCH AS SHE.

YOU ARE AND ALWAYS HAVE BEEN MY HEROINE!!

TO JOANNE FROM YOUR "LITTLE" BROTHER

WSE1

NOVEMBER 22, 1963

THEY LAUGHED AND CHEERED, THEY EVEN
JEERED
THE REASON I KNEW NOT WHY.
AND THEN THE NEWS, THE TRUTH WAS OUT
IT REALLY MADE ME CRY.

THE LAUGHTER WAS NOT FOR THE LIFE OF A MAN
NOR PEACE OR EVEN GOODWILL.
THEY CHEERED THE FACT OUR PRESIDENT
WAS THE VICTIM OF A KILL.

HOW SAD, I THOUGHT, THAT HUMAN BEINGS
COULD CARE SO LESS FOR ANOTHER.
"DIDN'T THEY KNOW?" I ASKED MYSELF,
"HE'S SOMEONE'S DAD AND BROTHER"?

WHAT WAS LOST THAT DAY, HISTORY WILL SAY
BROUGHT A NATION TOGETHER.
BUT THE LESSON I LEARNED ON THAT DARK DAY
WILL STAY WITH ME FOREVER

WSE1

NOVEMBER 22, 1963
COLUMBUS AIR FORCE BASE
COLUMBUS, MISSISSIPPI

RAY

WHAT CAN I SAY ABOUT MY GOOD FRIEND RAY
"IN A WORD... EXCELLENT," HE'LL ALWAYS SAY.

JOURNEYS... WE'VE SURE SHARED MANY
FUN... WE SURE HAD PLENTY

WE'VE HAD GREAT TIMES ALONG THE WAY
FROM TIJUANA TO SAN JOSE.

FOR HIS GOOD HEALTH I'LL ALWAYS PRAY
I'M GLAD TO HAVE MY GOOD FRIEND RAY!

WSE1

SITTIN' HERE THINKIN'

SITTIN' HERE THINKIN,' SMOKIN' AND DRINKIN'
CONCERNED ABOUT THE WORLD'S FATE.

ALL THIS KILLIN'... WE SHOULD BE CHILLIN'
WHY IS THERE SO MUCH HATE?

WE DON'T LIKE THIS, WE DON'T LIKE THAT
SOME LIKE NOTHING AT ALL.

IT'S SO DAMN HOT, IT'S SIZZLIN' OUTSIDE
CAN'T WAIT FOR THE SEASON CALLED "FALL."

POLITICS GETTIN' STRANGER AND STRANGER
ELECT THE WRONG ONE AND WE'RE ALL IN DAN-
GER.

COPS NEED TRAININ', SWAMPS NEED DRAININ'
THE BRIDGES AND HIGHWAYS ARE A MESS.

WE TALK ABOUT RIGHTS, FLAGS AND FIST-
FIGHTS
WHEN WE SHOULD BE DOING OUR BEST.

WSE1

SUMMER TIME

UP IN THE MORNING AND OUT TO PLAY
DON'T FORGET TO KNEEL AND PRAY.

HAVE PLENTY OF FUN AND LAUGH A LOT
AND THANK GOD FOR ALL YOU'VE GOT.

HIT THE BALL AND RUN THE BASES
WHILE DAYDREAMING OF BEAUTIFUL PLACES.

ENJOY YOUR FRIENDS UNTIL DAY IS DONE
YOU NEVER KNOW... YOU MIGHT LOSE ONE.

BACK IN THE HOUSE FOR DAILY BREAD
GIVE GOD PRAISE AND GO TO BED.

WSE1

THANKS

THANKS FOR THE LOVE YOU'VE GIVEN ME
AND THAT WE'VE YET TO SHARE.
THANKS FOR BEING WHO YOU ARE
AND TEACHING ME TO CARE.

THANKS TO YOU AGAIN MY LOVE
FOR THE HAPPINESS, JOY AND BLISS.
THANKS FOR THE SWEETEST LIPS
I'VE EVER CARED TO KISS.

THANKS FOR ALL YOUR EFFORTS
TO HELP ME REACH THE SKY.
'CAUSE IN MY HEART YOU'LL ALWAYS BE
MY DARLING "SWEETIE-PIE."

WSE1

THE MAN

OF MEN I OFTEN ASK MYSELF,
"WHAT MAKES A MAN A MAN?"
"WHO'S TO SAY," I ASK MYSELF,
"WHAT STANDARDS OUGHT DEMAND?"

A MAN'S A MAN TO THOSE WHO LOVE,
TO THOSE WHO LOVE AND CARE.
TO THOSE WHO NEED, TO THOSE WHO DOUBT,
TO THOSE WHO LOVE TO SHARE.

A MAN'S A MAN WHO'S FREE TO DO
AS OTHERS HAVE BEFORE,
TO ASK, TO SEEK, TO FIND,
TO WANDER THROUGH THAT DOOR.

A MAN'S A MAN WHO ACHES AND PAINS
WHO LAUGHS AND OFTEN CRIES.
A MAN IS ONE WHO LOOKS ABOVE
AND PENETRATES THE SKIES.

A MAN'S A MAN WHO PERCEIVES A THOUGHT
THAT OTHERS SURELY NEED.
A MAN IS ONE WHO NEED NOT ASK
HIS EMOTIONS TO BE FREED.

A MAN IS THIS AT LEAST,
AND SOMETHING MORE I SAY.
I ONLY HOPE I'LL BE A MAN
AND LIVE TO LIVE THAT DAY.

WSE1

THE NURSE

TWELVE HOUR SHIFTS
ARE JUST THE NORM
THEY GIVE US MEDS...
MAKE SURE WE'RE WARM.

A THANKLESS JOB
IN MANY WAYS
WORTH TWICE THE AMOUNT
IT USUALLY PAYS.

THERE WHEN YOU NEED THEM
THROUGH PAIN AND SCARES
THE NURSE IS THE ONE
WHO REALLY, REALLY CARES.

SO, WHEN YOU CLOSE YOUR EYES
TO PRAY AT NIGHT
INCLUDE THEM IN...
IT'S ONLY RIGHT.

ASK GOD TO BLESS THEM
AND HOLD THEM NEAR AND DEAR
DON'T KNOW WHAT WE'D DO
IF THEY WERE NOT HERE.

                         THANK YOU!!!

WSE1

THE RACE

HEADED IN DIFFERENT DIRECTIONS...
GOING TO THE SAME PLACE
SEEING WHO GETS THERE FIRST
TRYING TO WIN "THE RACE."

EAGER ON THE STARTING LINE
BRACED FOR THE START
LEAPING OVER HURDLES...
MATTERS OF THE HEART.

WE'RE COMING DOWN THE STRETCH NOW,
FINISH LINE IN SIGHT
WE'RE BOTH BREATHING HEAVY
HOPING THAT WE'RE RIGHT.

BAD TIME TO STUMBLE NOW...
WORST TIME TO FALL
YOU SEE THE WINNER LOSES EVERYTHING
THE LOSER TAKES IT ALL.

AND WHEN THE RACE IS OVER
AND THE WINNERS ARE DECLARED
WE'LL LOOK BACK IN RETROSPECT
AND WONDER HOW WE FARED.

YOU SEE, THE RACE IS ONE THAT'S HARD TO JUDGE,
VERY HARD TO CALL
IT MAKES YOU WONDER WHY WE CHOOSE
TO RUN THE RACE AT ALL.

WSE1

TO MY CHILDREN

IT'S BEEN SO LONG SINCE WE HAVE TALKED,
I THINK IT'S SUCH A SHAME
AND IF YOU LOOK WITHIN YOUR HEARTS...
I'M SURE THAT I'M TO BLAME.

WE SHARE MUCH MORE...
THAN JUST OUR LAST NAME
NO MATTER HOW LONG THAT WE'RE APART
I'LL LOVE YOU ALL THE SAME.

IF SAYING "I AM SORRY"
WOULD CHANGE THE WAY YOU FEEL
THEN LET ME SAY, "I AM SORRY"
...AND I MEAN THAT FOR REAL.

IF YOU FIND WITHIN YOUR HEARTS
TO SHARE YOUR LIVES WITH ME,
AND GIVE ME WHAT I'VE ALWAYS DREAMED...
A CLOSE-KNIT FAMILY.

I LOVE YOU AS I ALWAYS HAVE...
YOU MEAN SO MUCH TO ME
I HOPE THAT WE CAN LIVE OUR LIVES
IN PEACE AND HARMONY.

LOVE,
DAD

WSE1

TOM

MY BROTHER FROM ANOTHER MOTHER
THAT IS WHAT WE CALL EACH OTHER.

A SENSE OF HUMOR WE TEND TO SHARE
I MISS HIM MUCH WHEN HE'S NOT THERE.

THE JOY OF TIMES SPENT TOGETHER
WE ARE INDEED "BIRDS OF A FEATHER."

OUR VICES AND HABITS SEEM THE SAME
WILD AT TIMES, BUT NEVER TAME.

A REAL ARTIST WITH SPECIAL QUIRKS
WHEN IN "VEGAS" GO SEE HIS WORKS.

OUR LOVE FOR NATURE, ITS BEAUTY AND SOUNDS
WE'VE BEEN KNOWN TO HIT IT "OUT-OF-BOUNDS."

AND AS THROUGH LIFE WE CONTINUE TO WALK
I'LL LOVE MY BROTHER... THE ONE WITH THE HAWK.

LOVE YOU MY BROTHER!!

WSE1

TONY ("A.G.")

ALWAYS FAIR, NEVER PHONY
I LOVE MY FRIEND, HIS NAME IS TONY.

WE GO BACK NEARLY FIFTY YEARS
SO MUCH JOY... TOO MANY TEARS.

I'M HERE FOR HIM AS HE IS FOR ME
BROTHERS ARE WHAT WE'LL ALWAYS BE.

HE'S WATCHED ME CRY, HE'S MADE ME LAUGH
INTRODUCED ME TO "MY BETTER HALF."

AS WE AGE AND GROW REAL OLD
THERE'S STILL A STORY TO BE TOLD.

THE ADVENTURES WE SHARED, THE TIMES WE HAD
YET NO REGRETS... NO FEELING BAD.

WE'VE VISITED COUNTRIES, EIGHT IN ALL
DRANK TOO MUCH, BUT HAD A BALL.

WE WALKED THE PLANK OF A PIRATE SHIP,
WATCHED THE FRENCH "SKINNY-DIP."

AND THROUGH IT ALL WE ARE STILL HERE
A FRIENDSHIP THAT WE HOLD SO DEAR.

5/19/2016

WSE1

37

WANDA

SMART AS A WHIP
THE CAPTAIN OF HER SHIP

DEFINITELY THE OLDEST
MAYBE THE BOLDEST.

SHE'S MADE HER MARK ON THE WORLD
AND YET SHE'S STILL MY LITTLE GIRL.

I LOVE HER MUCH AND ALWAYS WILL
TO SEE HER FACE IS SUCH A THRILL.

SHE'S MY CONFIDANTE AND MY FRIEND
I LOVE HER TIL THE VERY END.

THANKS FOR BEING YOU.

WSE 1

WARREN

I LOVE HIM MUCH, HE'S MY SON
BORN THIRD BUT SECOND TO NONE.

MY CONFIDANT AND TRUSTED FRIEND
I PRAY HE'S THERE TO THE VERY END.

WHATEVER HE HAS HE GLADLY SHARES
IF YOU KNOW HIM WELL... HE TRULY
CARES.

HE LOVES HIS FAMILY... ONE AND ALL
NEED HIS HELP? ...PLACE THE CALL.

A BETTER MAN... YOU WON'T FIND ONE
I'M PROUD TO SAY HE'S MY SON.

WSE1

WHERE ARE WE GOING

WHERE ARE WE GOING?
WHERE DID WE COME FROM?
WHAT'S ALL THIS INJUSTICE?
WHY DID THEY SHOOT HIS SON?

I'VE WATCHED THEM DIE
FROM COWARD-FIRED SHOTS.
THE EMMITT TILLS,
THE ANWAR SADATS.

ALL GUNNED-DOWN BY THE SICK AND THE MEAN
MEDGAR EVERS, MARTIN LUTHER KING.

AND ALL THE OTHERS BEFORE AND SINCE
TRAGIC AFFAIRS... THE WORLD GROWS TENSE!!

WITH TERRORISTS, ASSASSINS,
KIDNAPS AND KILLINGS
BY MARTYRS WHO ALL
DIE SO WILLING.

THEY CARE LESS, THEY FEEL THE LEAST
THEY KILL THE WORLD'S MEN OF PEACE.

ALL THIS WITHOUT EVER KNOWING
THE DIRECTION IN WHICH THIS WORLD IS GOING.

WSE1

WILLIE

HE STUDIES HIS BIBLE WELL INTO THE NIGHT
MUST MAKE SURE THAT THE SERMON'S RIGHT.

HE STUDIES HARD
AND HONES HIS SKILLS OF CONVERSATION
THEN LAYS OUT THE TRUTH FOR THE CONGREGATION.

HE TELLS US STORIES OF PEACE AND GLEE
THEN LEADS THE CHOIR
SINGING "CLOSER TO THEE."

HE PRAYS FOR THE SICK AND THOSE IN NEED
AND WARNS US ALL AGAINST THE SIN OF GREED.

HE KNOWS THE COMMANDMENTS ONE THROUGH TEN
AND ASKS THE PEOPLE NOT TO SIN.

HE PRAYS FOR US DAYS ONE THROUGH SEVEN
TO HELP US FORGE AHEAD... ON OUR WAY TO HEAVEN.

HE KNOWS HIS BIBLE, BOTH CHAPTER AND VERSE
IF GOD IS THE DOCTOR
THEN SURELY, HE'S THE NURSE.

HE KNOWS MY NEEDS... LIKE NO OTHER
I'M SO GLAD TO CALL HIM MY BROTHER.

HIS GRACE AND LOVE HE WILL NOT HIDE
WE LOVE YOU MUCH, PASTOR PRIDE.

WSE1

WINNING

HERE WE SIT ALL SOAKED AND WET…
WON THE GAME BUT LOST THE BET.

WE PLAYED REAL HARD AND TRIED TO WIN
BUT THE OPPONENTS WON IN THE END.

BUT NEXT GAME COMES… WE'LL GIVE OUR ALL
WE'LL STAND OUR GROUND AND WIN THE BRAWL.

WE WON'T LET GO, WE'LL BUILD OUR HOPE
WE'LL KEEP OUR GRASP UPON THE ROPE.

WE'LL GIVE IT ALL WE'VE GOT… AND YET
WE MUST LOSE THE GAME TO WIN THE BET.

WSE1

YOU

THE ONE WHO TAUGHT US ALL A LESSON
NOTHING LESS THAN A HEAVENLY BLESSING.

YOU, THE ONE WHO SHARES SO MUCH LOVE
YOU, THE LAST ONE YOU'RE THINKING OF.

INSPIRATION TO ALL... CRITIC OF NONE
ROOM IN YOUR HEART FOR EVERYONE.

A PILLAR OF STRENGTH, A SYMBOL OF WHAT'S RIGHT
TAUGHT ME HOW TO LOVE AND WHEN TO FIGHT.

WSE1